Finally Liberated

Through the Reality of God's Love

ELEANOR STOCKERT

WESTBOW
PRESS®
A DIVISION OF THOMAS NELSON
& ZONDERVAN

WestBow Press books may be ordered through booksellers or by contacting:

WestBow Press
A Division of Thomas Nelson & Zondervan
1663 Liberty Drive
Bloomington, IN 47403
www.westbowpress.com
1 (866) 928-1240

Cover design by Patti Hughes

ISBN: 978-1-5127-7707-9 (sc)
ISBN: 978-1-5127-7706-2 (e)

Library of Congress Control Number: 2017902817

Print information available on the last page.

WestBow Press rev. date: 2/24/2017

Dedication

To Ernie, my husband of almost Sixty years,
who has always encouraged me to be all that God
called me to be and has set a great Christian
example for me to follow. I love you, Ernie!

Contents

Acknowledgments

To our daughter Patti Hughes for being there to help
me with all technical problems. Also for her artistic
abilities in designing the cover for this book.

Special Appreciation

To a wonderful friend, Marty Blair, who has been closer than a sister. She worked endless hours side by side with me to make this book a reality. Thank you, Marty!

Introduction

I've been a Christian for over twenty years now, and my walk with the Lord grows deeper and richer every year. But the first eight years of my walk were very different from what I am experiencing today. Looking back, I realize that as I was searching so hard for the truth, there was a major obstacle standing in my way. It was called "religious tradition," and it was being taught to me by people who really loved God and really loved me. Religious tradition acknowledges the deity of God, but denies His power. It says, "Jesus healed when He walked the earth, but not today." When a person is taught religious tradition, it becomes difficult to accept the truth of God's Word with childlike faith. Jesus Himself warned about this in Mark 7:13. He said that man can make the Word of God of no effect in his life through his traditions. Religious tradition came very close to stealing the truth of God's Word from my life.

When I accepted Jesus Christ as my Lord in 1975, He saved me out of a life so filled with despair, I was contemplating suicide. In 1958, at the age of nineteen, I had just given birth to our first daughter when suddenly, within a six-week period, four members of my family died. The death that had the greatest impact on me was that of my mother, who at age thirty-nine, took her own life. We had always been very close, and her suicide devastated me and plunged me into a very deep depression. Emotional problems plagued my life for the next sixteen years-until that night when

I asked Jesus to come into my life and He made everything new for me.

I had such a hunger to know Him that I would read the Bible day and night. I would get so excited over the goodness of God and the promises I found for my life. But when I went to church I would hear things that were contrary to what I had read. The pastor would say that if we disobeyed God He would send tests and trials to teach us a lesson so we would obey Him. One Sunday morning a man who had lost his arm in an accident stood up and gave a testimony of how God took his arm so that he would follow Him more closely. When I heard things like this, something inside me would say, "No, this is wrong." But then my head would say, "Look at these people––one is a pastor, the other a seasoned Christian–– surely they know more than me, a new convert." Yet the God I read about in the Bible did not do terrible things to people to get their attention. The Word says in Romans 2:4 that the goodness of God leads people to repentance.

What was being taught in this church (and is still being taught today in many churches) was based on the knowledge and traditions of men rather than on the knowledge of God's Word. The Word warns of the danger of such a practice. Hosea 4:8 states, "My people are destroyed because of lack of knowledge."

The Word explained to me what that "small voice" was inside of me that kept rejecting what these well-intentioned people were teaching. It was the Holy Spirit. Jesus said in John 4 that the Holy Spirit has been sent to "teach us all things." We should always listen to that small still voice down inside because it will prompt us to either receive or reject what we are being taught, depending on whether or not the teachings line up with the Word of God.

Two years after I accepted Jesus I went on a trip to Pennsylvania by myself to see my family. On the flight home I felt God wanted to say something to me. I was compelled to take a pen and write down the words "Finally Liberated." As I sat there trying to think what this could mean, the Lord spoke very clearly to me that I would someday write a book by this title. I remember thinking, *How could I ever do something like that?* But I just kept it in my heart all these years knowing that if God wanted me to write a book, He would show me when and how it was to be done.

Now eighteen years after that flight, having sat under the teaching of great men and women of God, I can clearly see what the Lord wants me to write. My greatest desire in writing this book is to share the truth from which perhaps all truth stems. That is, that God is ALL GOOD––full of love, compassion, and mercy. When you can receive that truth and begin to believe that goodness is directed toward you, all the promises found in His Word will come alive. As I look back on my walk with the Lord, I can see that the liberation I have experienced from my past is directly related to my willingness to believe in God's goodness. It is my prayer that as you read the pages that follow, you, too, will be able to turn from your past and lay hold of the promise of John 8:32, spoken by Jesus Himself . . .

> *And you shall know the truth, and the truth shall make you free.*

Our Father

"God is good all the time. And, all the time God is good." Every week our pastor ends our service with that simple statement. Yet, beneath the simplicity is a powerful truth that has too long either been ignored or denied by much of the Church––that is, that God is a good god, compassionate, loving, and merciful. Over the years, many in the body of Christ have looked to circumstances to explain what they don't understand, and as a result the character of God has been maligned. The Bible says in Mattrew 12:34, that out of the heart the mouth speaks. So, in order to know the heart of God (His will) you must know what He has already spoken through his Word. From Genesis to Revelation, the loving nature of God is revealed. He doesn't just *have* love, he *is* love. (I John 4:8). It was out of His desire to share His love that we were created. His love is so enduring that even when Adam sinned by disobeying Him, God immediately set into motion a plan to bring Man back into fellowship with Him. John 3:16 (amplified) states:

> *For God so greatly loved and dearly prized the world that*
> *He (even) gave up His only-begotten (unique) Son, so that*

> *whoever believes in (trusts, clings to, relies on) Him shall*
> *not perish (come to destruction, be lost), but have eternal*
> *(everlasting) life.*

One Sunday morning our pastor showed us a Scripture that literally changed my life. He read from John 17. Jesus is getting ready to go to the cross and is praying to the Father to keep all that had already come to Him and all that would come to Him in future generations. Vs. 22-23 (amp.) state:

> *I have given to them the glory and honor which You have*
> *given to Me, that they may be one, (even) as We are one,*
> *I in them and You in Me, in order that they may become*
> *one and perfectly united, that the world may know and*
> *(definitely) recognized that You sent Me, and that **You***
> ***have loved them (even) as You have loved Me.***

Realizing how much God loved me changed the way I looked at myself. I "felt" my value in God, and that enabled me to see myself as God saw me. I could now "love" myself, not because of who I was, but because of "whose" I was. The meaning of Mark 12:31 became clear. In that verse Jesus said we should love others as we love ourselves. By understanding and receiving the love God had for me, I was now able to give love to others more freely.

Realizing how much God loved me also changed my whole relationship with Him. Questions about whether God does bad things to people finally had answers––NO WAY! When I had a question about what God would or would not do, I would change the question to "What would 'love' do in this situation?" Knowing that God loved me so much took away all the fear that He would ever do anything that would hurt me. In John 4:18 (amp.) it says,

> *There is no fear in love—dread does not exist; but full-*
> *grown (complete, perfect) love turns fear out of doors and*

expels every trace of terror! For fear brings with it the thought of punishment, and (so) he who is afraid has not reached the full maturity of love——is not yet grown into love's complete perfect.

The Lord wants so much to bless His children and show Himself strong on their behalf, but in order for Him to do this we must get acquainted with Him so we can know what we can expect Him to do. Isaiah 55:8-9 says that God's ways are higher and different from our ways, so we need to learn "His ways." Let's take a close look at the attributes a good earthly father would be expected to possess and compare them to the attributes of our Heavenly Father as revealed in His Word.

Earthly Father	Heavenly Father
He wanted a child from the very beginning.	God chose us in Christ before the foundation of the world. (Ephesians 1:4)
He stayed very close to the mother of his child as she carried the child in her womb.	God formed my inward parts; He covered me in my mother's womb. (Psalms 139:13)
He wants a good life for his child.	Jesus said that He came that you might have life more abundantly. (John 10:10)
He is a man of his word.	God has magnified His Word above His Name. (Psalms 138:2)
He is honest.	God cannot lie. (Titus 1:2)

Earthly Father	Heavenly Father
He is stable (consistent).	Every good gift and every perfect gift is from above, and comes down from the Father of lights, with whom there is no variation or shadow of turning. (James 1:17)
	Jesus is the same yesterday, today and forever. (Hebrews13:8)
He is always available.	He who keeps you will not slumber. (Psalms121:3)
	Let us therefore come boldly to the throne of grace, that we may obtain mercy and find grace to help in time of need. (Hebrews4:16)
He helps his child out of trouble.	Many are the afflictions of the righteous, but the Lord delivers him out of them all. (Psalms34:19)
He protects his child.	No evil shall befall you, nor shall any plague come nigh your dwelling; for God has given His angels charge over you. (Psalms91:10-11)

Earthly Father	Heavenly Father
He corrects and teaches his child.	All scripture is given by inspiration of God, and is profitable for doctrine, for reproof, for correction in righteousness. (2 Timothy 3:16)
He guides his child.	The steps of a good man are ordered by the Lord. (Psalms 37:23)
He believes in his child.	He said I could do all things through Christ. (Philippians 4:13)
He is always interested in the smallest detail of his child's life.	God has numbered every hair on your head. (Matthew 10:30)
He is pleased when his child does good.	God takes pleasure in the prosperity of His servant. (Psalms 35:27)
He tells his child not to worry, that he'll take care of everything.	Cast all your care on Him, for He cares for you. (1 Peter 5:7)
He gives his child shelter.	For You have been a shelter unto me, a strong tower from my enemy. (Psalms 61:3)

Earthly Father	Heavenly Father
He gives his child food.	God give us our daily bread. (Matthew6:11)
He is compassionate.	As a father loves and pities his children, so the Lord loves and pities those who fear Him–– with reverence, worship, and awe. (Psalms 103:13) (amp.)
He looks after his child's health.	God says we are healed by the stripes of Jesus. (1 Peter 2:24)
He rescues his child.	Look up for your redemption draws nigh. (Luke 21:28)
He always wants to be near his child.	Jesus said He's going to prepare a place for you, to be with Him and the Father forever. (John 14:1-3)

Picture in your mind a man walking with his young son. The father is very tall and strong, and the boy is very tiny alongside his dad. As the boy looks up to his father you sense the pride, the great love, and respect he has for him. As long as the boy holds his father's hand, he knows without a doubt that nothing could ever harm him. That's the way we need to be with our Father God. We need to look up to Him with all our love and respect and need to honor Him and His Word. Then we can walk securely in these dangerous days we are living and know that our hand is held firmly by our Father's Hand.

God loves you so much! He has written you a love letter––the

Bible—that describes from beginning to end His unfailing love for you. Chapter by chapter He reveals the provisions He has given his children to provide a way for them to be victorious in life. In 2 Peter 1:3 we are told that He has given to us "all things that pertain to life and godliness, *through the knowledge of Him* who called us by glory and virtue." Notice it says through "the knowledge of Him." The only way to receive this knowledge is to become a disciple of God's Word. Disciple in the Greek means a learner, a student. Determine now to become a student of God's Word. Get to know your Heavenly Father and you will quickly discover that to know Him is to love Him, and you will never again doubt that . . .

God is good all the time. And, all the time God is good.

The Love of God

Probably the one attribute of God that the world—and even the Church—stumbles over more than any other is the "Love of God." Many people have no problem with God being "everywhere present," (omnipresent), or being "all powerful," (omnipotent), but when He is described as "all loving," it just seems too much for many to believe. But that is exactly what the Word says in 1 John 4:8 God is love." The nature of that love is described in 1 Corinthians 13:4-8 (amp.):

> *Love endures long and is patient and kind; love is never envious nor boils over with jealousy; is not boastful or vainglorious, does not display itself haughtily. It is not conceited—arrogant and inflated with pride; it is not rude (unmannerly), and does not act unbecomingly. Love (God's love in us) does not insist on its own rights or its own way, for it is not self-seeking; it is not touchy or fretful or resentful; it takes no account of the evil done to it—pays no attention to a suffered wrong. It does not rejoice at injustice and unrighteousness, but rejoices when right and truth prevail. Love bears up*

under anything and everything that comes; is ever ready to believe the best of every person; its hopes are fadeless under all circumstances and it endures everything (without weakening). Love never fails—never fades out or becomes obsolete or comes to an end.

Yet for so long much of the Church has viewed God from the world's perspective. They see Him as a stern God, ready and eager to jump on people's mistakes and teach them lessons through "tests and trials." People do believe in the love of God, in that once a person has suffered enough, God delivers him out of his trial. Where did this idea originate? I believe in the mind of Satan. He knows that if he can keep the world—and especially the Church—divided over this issue, he can stop God's Word from coming to pass in the earth. Up to now he has done a pretty effective job of deceiving people about God's nature.

In the world Satan has managed to get governments and some of the most powerful businesses in the world—insurance companies—to legally declare disasters such as hurricanes and earthquakes as "acts of God." But they are not acts of the God of the Bible, but rather acts of Satan, whose only power is that of deception. Satan has been almost as effective in deceiving the Church. For every one person who will share the healing power of God's Word with a sick person, there are two or three people there to tell the person, "Just hang in there; God's trying to teach you something."

Receiving God's love into our lives affects us in two very important ways. The first way is that God's love opens our eyes to our need of Him. Romans 2:4 says that it is the *goodness of God* that leads people to repentance. Receiving His "love" opens the door to being born-again, which, in turn, opens the door to all the other blessings of God. The second way in which the love of God affects us is to open our eyes to the wonderful life he has planned for us on *this side* of heaven. God has a divine destiny for each of his children. Because the potential God sees in us is far greater than the potential we can ever see in ourselves, it is important to have the right image of Him and ourselves as He sees us. Having that right image then allows us to discover His perfect will for our lives.

It is only through God's Word that we will be able to get the right image of God and of ourselves. As we find out what the Word has to say, we must be prepared to accept what is said by faith, because our minds cannot naturally comprehend the image provided in the Word. As we go through His Word we must pay close attention to those verses that tell us "who we are in Christ," "what is ours in Christ," and "what we are capable of doing in Christ." We must meditate on these scriptures until they become big on the inside of us (and then continue to meditate on them so they *stay* big on the inside of us). When our minds are renewed with these scriptures, we are then able to step out in faith and claim the wonderful promises God has provided for us.

In both the Old and the New Testaments the heart of God is poured out in His Word. Jeremiah 29:11 states God's desire for us: "For I know the thoughts that I think toward you," says the Lord, "thoughts of peace and not of evil, to give you a future and a hope." In 3 John 2 it says the same thing, but only in a different way: "Beloved, I pray above all things that you may prosper in all things and be in health just as your soul prospers."

As you begin to believe the truth of God's love and come to the point where you realize He is *one hundred percent* behind you, you will be able to begin walking in the destiny He has for you. And that destiny will lead you to a life of loving and helping others to likewise discover the joy of His love.

It is such a privilege to worship God and to be called His very own. That is what the love of God is really all about––being God's "own." It is about meaning so much to Him that: 1) in the beginning, He created us out of a desire to have fellowship with us, and 2) when we were separated from Him by sin, He bought us back with the shed blood of His Son. That is the love revealed in 1 John 3:1.

Behold what manner of love the Father has bestowed on us, that we should be called children of God!

Come as Children . . .
Follow as Sheep

The Bible refers to believers as children. Jesus said in Matthew 18:34 (amp.):

> *Truly I say to you, unless you repent (change, turn about) and become like little children (trusting, lowly, loving, and forgiving) you can never enter the kingdom of heaven at all. Whoever will humble himself therefore and becomes as a little child (trusting, lowly, loving, and forgiving) is greatest in the kingdom of heaven."*

Think for a moment what distinguishes a child from an adult (other than the obvious differences in age and size). The primary difference is the way in which a child responds to the cares of life. For the most part, a child has none. And on those occasions when he has a concern, the child immediately runs to his father, knowing he will take care of it. Who but a child can one minute be crying in his father's arms about a situation, and the next minute be running off with a big smile on his face to play, crisis resolved? In short, a child knows where to get his needs met. A child looks to his father with absolute trust in his ability to handle any problem, to fulfill any promise.

When a father promises to buy his son a new bike, the response is very predictable. The child jumps up and down with glee, and spends most of his waking hours thinking and talking about the new bike. When his father brings the new bike home, the child's reaction is one of elation. He pours out his love and gratitude on his father and his father, in turn, feels a special joy at having been able to provide his child with something that he wanted.

Consider, on the other hand, how the situation would have changed if the son had not trusted his father to fulfill the promise of a new bike. The effect on both the father and son would have been very different. The son would have had no peace. He would have spent his time worrying and fretting about what his father "wasn't going to do for him." His father would have been hurt because his son did not trust him. Moreover, the father would have been grieved because his son was not walking in the level of excitement and anticipation that should have accompanied the promise of a new bike.

This is how it is all too frequently with us as believers. God gives us a promise in his Word and we don't believe Him to deliver on that promise. We do just the opposite through our words and our actions. If someone accused us of calling God a liar, we would vehemently deny it. Yet the way we respond to God's Word betrays us. It is only when we choose to rely on our heavenly Father with the same absolute trust that a child has for his earthly father that we open the door for His promises to be fulfilled in our lives.

God's Word also refers to believers as sheep. The most noticeable characteristic of sheep is their total reliance on the shepherd. Sheep are so "in touch" with their shepherd they respond to the sound of his voice. God has given believers the Holy Spirit as "His voice" to which we can respond. When we learn to respond to that "inner witness" as readily as sheep respond to their shepherd, we will begin to see our needs and wants met. This is the picture the Lord created in Psalm 23 (amp.).

Verse 1: "The Lord is my shepherd (to feed, guide, and shield me). I shall not lack." God is a God of total supply. (Philippians 4:19) (amp.) says, "and my God will liberally supply (fill to the full) your EVERY need according to His riches in glory in Christ Jesus."

Verse 2: "He makes me lie down in green (fresh, tender) pastures; He leads me beside the still and restful waters." Jesus is the Prince of Peace (Isaiah 9:6). Jesus said in John 14:27 (amp.), "Peace I leave you; my (own) peace I now give and bequeath to you. Not as the world gives do I give to you. Do not let your heart be troubled, neither let it be afraid—stop allowing yourselves to be agitated and disturbed; and do not permit yourselves to be fearful and intimidated and cowardly and unsettled."

Verse 3: "He refreshes and restores my life—my self; He leads me in the paths of righteousness (uprightness and right standing with Him—not for my earning it; but) for His name's sake." Jesus is our guide. Psalms 37:23 (amp.) states: The steps of a (good) man are directed and established of the Lord, when He delights in his way (and He busies Himself with his every step).

Verse 4: "Yes, though I walk through the (deep, sunless) valley of the shadow of death, I will fear or dread no evil; for you are with me; your rod (to

protect) and your staff (to guide), they comfort me."
Hebrews 13:5 (amp.) states, "(God) Himself has
said, "I will not in any way fail you or give you up
nor leave you without support. (I will) not, (I will)
not (I will) not in any degree leave you helpless,
nor forsake nor let (you) down, (relax) my hold on
you––ASSUREDLY NOT!" When we *believe* that
Jesus has hold of our lives like this, we can make it
through the darkest hours of any storm.

Verse 5: "You prepare a table before me in the
presence of my enemies; You anoint my head with
oil; my brimming cup runs over." God has given
us His armor to defeat our enemies. Ephesians
6:10-11 (amp.) states, "In conclusion, be strong in
the Lord––be empowered through your union
with Him; draw your strength from Him (that
strength which His boundless might provides). Put
on God's whole armor––the armor of a heavily-
armed soldier, which God supplies––that you may
be able to successfully stand up against (all) the
STRATEGIES and deceits of the devil." God has
also given us His Holy Spirit to empower us. Jesus
said in Acts 1:8 (amp.), "But you shall receive power,
ability, efficiency, and might when the Holy Spirit
has come upon you, and you shall be witnesses to
me in Jerusalem, and in Judea and Samaria, and to
the end of the earth."

Verse 6: "Surely only goodness, mercy, and
unfailing love shall follow me all the days of my
life; and through the length of days the house of the
Lord (and His presence) shall be my dwelling place."

This is God's perfect will for every one of his children—total trust and reliance on Him for every need to be met. When this happens a life full of joy and victory becomes possible. Psalms 16:11 (amp.) says, "You will show me the path of life; in Your presence is fullness of joy, at Your right hand there are pleasures for evermore."

The behavior of both children and sheep brings to mind two essential elements that believers must have in their walk with the Lord in order to enjoy the fullness of His blessings—trust and dependence. Psalms 91:2 (amp.) states, "I will say of the Lord, He is my refuge and my fortress, my God, on Him I lean and rely, and in Him I (confidently) trust." God's love is available to all men, but His blessings are poured out in abundance only on those who choose to **take Him at His Word!**

Rock or Sand Castle?

There is such confusion in the world today. Every area of life seems to be heading toward chaos. We live in a society where the number one rule for many is "There are no rules." We are led by government officials, many of whom have a difficult time adhering to the very laws they have sworn to uphold. We live under a justice system which many times seems to show more concern for the criminal than for the victim of the crime. We have an economic system where many of the programs designed to help people get back on their feet actually encourage them to remain dependent on the government. Even the weather patterns seem to be in upheaval.

The Bible has a lot to say about the times in which we live. Many Bible scholars believe that we are living in what the Word of God refers to as the "last days." 2 Timothy 3:1-5 (amp.) says,

> But understand this, that in the last days there will come (set in) perilous times of great stress and trouble—hard to deal with and hard to bear. For people will be lovers of self and (utterly) self-centered, lovers of money and aroused by an inordinate (greedy) desire for wealth,

proud and arrogant and contemptuous boasters. They will be abusive (blasphemous, scoffers), disobedient to parents, ungrateful, unholy, and profane. (They will be) without natural (human) affection (callous and inhuman), relentless——admitting of no truce or appeasement. (They will be) slanderers——false accusers, trouble makers; intemperate and loose in morals and conduct, uncontrolled and fierce, haters of good. (They will be) lovers of sensual pleasures and vain amusements more than and rather than lovers of God. For (although) they hold a form of piety (true religion), they deny and reject and are strangers to the power of it——their conduct belies the genuineness of their profession. Avoid (all) such people——turn away from them.

God's Word not only describes the chaos of the last days, it also provides the answer to living in a time like this. In Matthew 7:24-26 (amp.), Jesus is warning us to look to God's Word and to obey it so we won't be destroyed with other people who don't know God or who don't want to walk in His ways.

So everyone who hears these words of Mine and acts upon them——obeying them——will be like a sensible (prudent, practical, wise) man who built his house upon the rock; and the rain fell and the floods came, and the winds blew and beat against that house, but it did not fall, because it had been founded on the rock. And everyone who hears these words of Mine and does not do them will be like a stupid (foolish) man who built his house upon the sand; and the winds blew and beat against that house, and it fell.

Notice the similarities of the two examples given. Both had houses and both houses were hit by the same storm. The difference was in the foundation on which each house was built. One was built on the rock—God's Word, the other on the sand—the world's way. Jesus is showing us the choice that is before us. We can look to Him through God's Word and find safety in all the storms that surround us in life, or we can be like the foolish man and look to the world for answers that never quite go far enough.

It is a shame that in a time when we need to totally trust God, so many people are placing their faith in the things of this world. For many, "trust" is established with a good paycheck and job security. Yet too many people are finding that these things can be "here today, gone tomorrow." For others, a good health plan is the measuring stick for security. However, not even the best health plan provides much security when the doctors say there is nothing more that they can do. Certainly paychecks and health care plans are important in life. But they provide limited answers to life's seemingly limitless challenges. That is why it is essential to know what God's Word says. His Word will continue when all other things have ceased.

The Word of God has the answer for every challenge that can come our way in this world. In the area of finances, for instance, the Lord has a lot to say. In Luke 12:21-31, Jesus is saying that man is not to store up treasures on earth, but that his riches should be in his relationship with God. He tells us not to be worried about the material needs of everyday life, but to trust our Heavenly Father to take care of our every need. Jesus tells us where our focus is to be in Matthew 6:33: "Seek ye first the kingdom of God and His righteousness, and all these things shall be added unto you."

We see God's desire for His people in the financial and physical realm in 3 John 2 (amp.):

> Beloved, I pray that you may prosper in every way and (that your body) may keep well, even as (I know) your soul keeps well and prospers.

Your soul (mind, will, and emotions) can only prosper in one way—by being transformed by the Word of God. What does the Word say about unlocking the material blessings His Word says He desires us to have? In Malachi 3:10, the Lord gives us very clear direction:

> *Bring all the tithes—the whole tenth of your income—*
> *into the storehouse (church) that there may be food in My*
> *House, and prove Me now by it, says the Lord of Hosts, if*
> *I will not open the windows of Heaven for you and pour*
> *you out a blessing, that there shall not be room enough*
> *to receive it.*

What a deal! In return for our giving ten percent of our income, we have the right to believe God will supernaturally bless the remaining ninety percent. Remember, God does not need our money, but he choose to use that ten percent as an avenue through which to bless those who are willing to trust Him to do what He said He would do.

Just as knowledge of God's Word concerning prosperity opens the door for financial security, knowledge of God's Word concerning all other areas of our life is necessary to live victoriously in this increasingly chaotic world. Hosea 4:6 warns of the high price to be paid for ignorance: "My people perish because of lack of knowledge" Knowing the Word of God and choosing to act on it is like the man who built his house on the rock. When the storm came the house stood. You, too, can remain standing through your storm. Start building your foundation on *"The Rock"* today!

Protect Your Heart

Psalms 139:14 states, "I will praise thee for I am fearfully and wonderfully made" Indeed, we are God's crowning creation. We know from Genesis that we are created in His image. And just as God is a three-part being, so are we––spirit, soul, and body. We are a spirit, we have a soul, and we operate through a body. The spirit, often referred to as the "heart" (not the blood pump) in the Bible is the "real you." This is where the kingdom of God resides in a believer. It is the part of you that was changed or "born-again" in an instant when you made Jesus the Lord of your life. Of our three-part being, only our spirit was changed immediately by the new birth. The other two parts––the body and the soul––will only be changed by an ongoing transformation process. (Romans 12:2)

The devil cannot *directly* touch your spirit once it has been reborn. He can only *indirectly* affect your spirit through the pressure he applies to your soul (made up of your will, mind, and emotions) and your body. Man is connected to this world by five physical senses. They are constantly relaying information to our minds. Our minds are like a computer––they store information. Through the process of recall we can go over and over information that we have stored in our minds. That can be very good if it is something that we need to remember. But it can be harmful if it is something like a television program that is full of violence and murder, because it can produce fear as we think about it over and over again. The Bible warns us not to subject ourselves to negative things, but rather to think of good things. (Philippians 4:8)

The enemy is working overtime to get control of you through your body and mind. Everywhere we look in society today there are things luring us away from God and into the enemy's camp. The language, the violence, the sexually-explicit scenes on television and in the movies alone just scratch the surface of the things the devil has devised to distract us. The advancement of the abortion movement and the homosexual movement in our society reflect just how far we have strayed from Godly principles as we move toward the 21st century. James 4:4 (amp.) states the Lord's view without compromise: "Do you not know that being the world's friend is being God's enemy? So whoever chooses to be a friend of the world takes his stand as an enemy of God."

God designed our hearts to receive His Word so that our lives would be filled with His blessings in order that we could carry the Gospel (His love and deliverance) to a dying world. For this reason, Proverbs 4:23 admonishes us to guard our hearts, for out of it flow the issues of life. When our hearts are nourished with His Word, we are able to overcome any attack from the enemy, regardless of whether it is leveled against our spirit, soul, or body.

Jesus teaches us the importance of nourishing and guarding our hearts in Mark 4. He explains it through the following parable, verses 3-8:

> *Hearken; Behold, there went out a sower to sow: And it came to pass, as he sowed, some fell by the wayside, and the fowls of the air came and devoured it up. And some fell on the stony ground, where it had not much earth; and immediately it sprang up, because it had no depth*

*of earth: but when the sun was up, it was scorched; and
because it had no root, it withered away. And some fell
among thorns, and the thorns grew up and choked it,
and it yielded no fruit. And other fell on good ground,
and did yield fruit that sprang up and increased; and
brought forth, some thirty, and some sixty, and some
a hundred.*

In this parable the ground represents the heart of man and the seed represents the Word of God. The entire parable surrounds the condition of the ground (heart), not the seed, because the Word is pure (Proverbs 30:5) and endures forever (1 Peter 1:25). In Mark 4:14 Jesus begins to explain the parable to his disciples: "The sower sows the word." The Word of God can be sown many different ways—through a pastor, a Bible study group, teaching tapes, a book, or a television ministry. Jesus goes on to discuss four groups of people that are as much a part of our world today as they were when Jesus taught this parable. Verse 15 describes the first group of people to hear the Word. "These are they by the wayside where the word is sown; but when they have heard, Satan cometh immediately, and taketh away the Word that was sown in their hearts." These are the "wayside" people. They are those who just stumble onto the Word. They hear it, but use their reasoning to try to understand it. This causes doubt and unbelief to rise up and Satan comes immediately and steals the Word that had been scattered in their hearts.

The second group of people are described in vs. 16-17. "And these are they likewise which are sown on stony ground; who, when they have heard the Word, immediately receive it with gladness; And have no root in themselves, and so endure but for a time: afterward, when affliction or persecution ariseth for the Word's sake, immediately they are offended." These are the "stony-hearted" people. These are those who seek out the Word and receive it gladly. But they don't take time to allow the Word to grow, and when Satan brings persecution and tribulation because of the Word that has been sown in their lives, they become offended (i.e., "I tried what the Word said to do and it didn't work for me!)"

Vs. 18-19 reveal a third group of people. "And these are they which are sown among thorns; such as hear the Word, and the cares of this world, and the deceitfulness of riches, and the lusts of other things entering in, choke the Word, and it becometh unfruitful." The "thorny people" are a very sad group. These are people who want the things of God. The Word is beginning to grow in their lives. But the "weeds of life"—the cares of the world (worry), the deceitfulness of riches (money is not the problem, the love of money is), and other things (anything that keeps you from spending time in the Word), choke off their spiritual growth. This group experiences a crop failure.

The fourth group of people is the group that we all want to be a part of. They are described in v. 20. "And these are they which are sown on good ground; such as hear the Word, and receive it, and bring forth fruit, some thirty-fold, some sixty, and some a hundred." These are the "good-ground" people—"the doers of the Word, not hearers only." They hear the Word, receive it, and experience a mighty harvest from the seed sown into their lives. These people are totally sold out to the Lord. They are patient and willing to pay any price to receive the Kingdom of God into their lives. Mattrew 11:11-12 (amp.) states,

> Truly, I tell you, among those born of women there has not risen one greater than John the Baptist; yet he who is least in the kingdom of heaven is greater than he. And from the days of John the Baptist until the present time the kingdom of heaven has endured violent assault, and violent men seize it by force (as a precious prize) a share in the heavenly kingdom is sought for with most ardent zeal and intense exertion.

In Mark 4:13, Jesus says that if you understand the parable of the sower, you'll understand all the parables. He also says that nothing is hidden that won't be revealed. Jesus is telling us that if we take heed to what we hear––by putting it in our hearts and meditating on it until we "know that we know that we know"––more understanding will be given to us. The ways of God are a mystery to the world and only those who are completely sold out to Him will understand His ways. Remember, the things of God are hidden in His Word *for us* not to be kept *from us* (Mark 4:22).

When we see the significance Jesus placed on the parable of the sower, it is easy to see why the enemy attacks every time the Word goes forth. If a person receives the truth of that parable the door is opened to understand the countless other truths hidden in God's Word. So when Satan comes to steal the Word from our hearts by sowing thoughts of doubt and unbelief we must respond immediately with what the Word says. Philippians 4:13 (amp.) says, "I have strength for all things in Christ who empowers me––I am ready for anything and equal to anything through Him who infuses inner strength into me, (that is, I am self-sufficient in Christ's sufficiency.)" When we hide this verse in our heart and the full truth explodes within us, we are well on our way to becoming "hundred-fold" Christians. The Word gives us an example of one such person in Psalm 1. The person described there should be a role model for us all. He is the one who is not only blessed but because of the blessings he enjoys, he can be a blessing to others. He is the one who has the answer for a dying world. He is the one who "protects his heart!":

> *His delight and desire are in the law of the Lord, and on*
> *His law––the precepts, the instructions, the teachings*
> *of God––he habitually meditates (ponders and studies)*
> *by day and by night. And he shall be like a tree firmly*
> *planted (and tended) by the streams of water, ready to*
> *bring forth his fruit in its season; his leaf also shall not*
> *fade or wither, and everything he does shall prosper (and*
> *come to maturity). Psalms 1:2-3 (amp.)*

Heed Your Words

"Sticks and stones may break your bones, but words can never hurt you." How many times did we hear that adage when we were growing up? While those who told us that had our best interest in mind, from a Biblical standpoint nothing could be further from the truth. Proverbs 18:21 (amp.) states, "Death and life are in the power of the tongue, and they who indulge in it shall eat the fruit of it (life or death)." According to God's Word then, our success or defeat in any area of our lives is dependent on our words. James 3:2 (amp.) says that the perfect man is one who does not stumble in word because he bridles his whole body by controlling his tongue. V. 3-6 (amp.) go on to explain in depth the importance of controlling what comes out of our mouths:

> If we set bits in horses' mouths to make them obey us, we can turn their whole bodies about. Likewise look at the ships, though they are so great and are driven by rough winds, they are steered by a very small rudder wherever the impulse of the helmsman determines. Even so the tongue is a little member, and it can boast of

*great things. See how much wood or how great a forest
a tiny spark can set ablaze! And the tongue is a fire.
(The tongue is a) world of wickedness set among our
members, contaminating and depraving the whole body
and setting on fire the wheel of birth—the cycle of man's
nature—being itself ignited by hell.*

To fully understand the power of words we must go back to the
book of Genesis. There we find that "words" are what God used
to create all that exists today. Genesis 1:3 says, "Then God *said*,
Let there be light; and there was light." Read the first chapter of
Genesis and note the number of times the word "said" is used and
the number of "creations" that resulted.

The world may not acknowledge the power of words because of
what the Bible says, but it recognizes the impact that words have in
the development of our lives. Psychiatrists and psychologists warn
of the damage that can result when the wrong kind of words are
spoken to a child. Statements like, "You're stupid," "You'll never
amount to anything," or "I'm sorry you were ever born," may be
said in a moment of anger, but the echo of such statements lives on
inside a child for the rest of his life and may ultimately destroy his
spirit. Proverbs 15:4 (amp.) confirms this. "A gentle tongue (with its
healing power) is a tree of life, but a willful contrariness in it breaks
down the spirit."

How can words be so devastating when God's original intent
was to use words to create good? It is because for every truth found
in God's Word, the devil has come up with a counterfeit to pervert
that truth. He has perverted the creative power God gave to words
to produce evil. In God's Kingdom, if you mix words with faith,
something good is created, because the spirit world responds to
what you have spoken. In Satan's kingdom, if you mix words with
fear, something bad is created. Once again the spirit world has
responded. Because many Christians have little idea of what the
Word says about the importance of what comes out of our mouths,

the enemy is very successful at getting people to agree with him by what they say.

It is sad that the world and many in the Church believe there is some kind of a "demilitarized zone" between God's Kingdom and Satan's. They think as long as they stay in the middle they won't be affected by spiritual things. Yet the Word is quite clear in Colossians 1:13 that there are two kingdoms and you are either in one or the other. When you are delivered from one to the other there is no "demilitarized zone" that you can settle in. Believers need to understand that if their words are not firmly rooted in God's Word, then by *default*, they are rooted in enemy territory. Let's look at some of the all-too-familiar phrases used in our society today: "My back's killing me," "These doctor bills are going to send us to the poor house," "I was scared to death." A person may say any of these statements in a flippant manner, maybe just to get a response from the person with whom they are talking. Yet the spirit world does not act on what they mean; it simply responds to the words spoken. This is not to say you can never express a problem that exists. It is fine to say, "My back is hurting," and then add, "but praise God, I believe I receive my healing based on 1 Peter 2:24." The Word says that Jesus is our High Priest (Hebrews 4:14) and that He is always there to intercede on our behalf (Hebrews 7:25). He cannot act on our behalf if our words are filled with doubt and fear. But He can act on our behalf when we speak His Word over the situation. Paul gave us some specific guidelines to follow in choosing our words. In Ephesians 4:29 (amp.) he says,

> *"Let no foul or polluting language, nor evil word, nor unwholesome or worthless talk (ever) come out of your mouth: but only such (speech) as is good and beneficial to the spiritual progress of others, as is fitting to the need and the occasion, that it may be a blessing and give grace (God's favor) to those who hear it."*

Because words "create," it is very important that we know the right words to speak. That means having an ever-increasing knowledge of the Word of God in our lives. What is on the inside of us is eventually going to come out in the words we speak. So we must study so that the Word becomes a part of us. Jesus confirms this in Matthew 12:34-37 (amp.):

> For out of the fullness (the overflow, the superabundance) of the heart the mouth speaks. The good man from his inner good treasure flings forth good things, and the evil man out of his inner evil storehouse flings forth evil things. But I tell you on the day of judgment men will have to give account for every idle (inoperative, non-working) word they speak. For by your words you will be justified and acquitted, and by our words you will be condemned and sentenced.

Words that carry forth faith, love, and hope come from God. Words of fear, lack, and worry come from the devil. We are the ones who bring either the Lord and His blessings into our lives or the devil and his misery into our lives by the words we speak. So begin now to think about the words you speak. Say only those things that line up with what God says in His Word. Making this choice will open the door to the favor of God not only in your life but in the lives of future generations of your family. God promises this in Deuteronomy 30:19. It is a promise for those who choose their words carefully.

> I call Heaven and Earth to witness this day against you, that I have set before you life and death, the blessing and the curse; therefore choose life, that you and your descendants may live.

Know Your Enemy . . . Know Your Authority Over Him

Satan is a defeated foe. He was completely stripped of his power as a result of Jesus' death burial, and resurrection. Colossions 2:15 says, "Having disarmed principalities and powers, He made a public spectacle of them, triumphing over them in it." After dying on the Cross, Jesus descended into hell and took back the authority that Satan had been given as a result of Adam and Eve's transgression. Jesus spoke of that fact in Revelation 1:17-18. He said, "Do not be afraid; I am He who lives, and was dead, and behold I am alive forevermore. Amen. And I have the keys of Hades and of death." Keys represent authority. This was a fulfillment of what Jesus had spoken of in Matthew 16:18-19, where he was speaking about the authority the Church would have as a result of His sacrifice:

> *That the gates of Hell would not prevail against the church. And I will give you the keys of the Kingdom of Heaven, and whatsoever you bind on earth will be bound in Heaven; and whatever you loose on earth will be loosed in Heaven.*

Having gone to the Cross, Jesus once again spoke of the authority He had purchased for the Church, just prior to returning to His Father. In Matthew 28:18-20 He said,

> *All authority has been given to Me in Heaven and on Earth. Go therefore and make disciples of all nations, baptizing in the name of the Father, Son, and Holy Spirit, teaching them to observe all things that I have commanded you; and lo, I am with you always, even until the end of the age.*

Although it is a Biblical fact that Satan is a defeated foe, it is also a fact that he is still exerting power throughout the earth today, as an outlaw. Putting it in natural terms, we know that it is against the law to rob a bank. Bank robbers have no right to do what they do, but unless they are stopped by someone in authority (law enforcement officers), they can continue to rob banks and get away with it. The same is true with Satan. He has no right to do what he does, but unless there is a believer willing to enforce his defeat, he can continue on his destructive ways.

Satan has numerous devices he uses to bring defeat and destruction throughout the world. All of them revolve around his number one desire, which is to cause people to *doubt God*—to doubt that He exists, to doubt that He means what He says, and to doubt that He will do what He says He will do in His Word. His tactics are to intimidate (1 Peter 5:8), to accuse (Revelation 12:10), to tempt (Luke 4:5-6), to deceive (2 Corinthians 4:3-4), to divide (Matthew 12:25), and to confuse (James 3:16).

A look at the way Satan operated in the days of Adam and Eve will reveal to us the way he still operates today. As mentioned, his primary goal is to create *doubt*. He first achieved this goal in the Garden of Eden, where Adam and Eve gave away all God had created for them. Genesis 1:28 (amp.) reveals the extent of authority God had given man:

And God blessed them, and said to them, 'Be fruitful,
multiply, and fill the earth and subdue it (with all its
vast resources); and have dominion over the fish of the
sea, the birds of the air, and over every living creature
that moves upon the earth.

I really believe God had the devil in mind when he made this statement. Unfortunately, that authority did not remain in the hands of man for long. Satan came into the Garden as a serpent and sowed his seeds of doubt. In Genesis 3:1 the serpent said, "Has God indeed said, 'You shall not eat of every tree of the garden?'" In effect he was saying, "Are you sure God meant what he said?" He was able to get Eve to question God, then she got Adam to go along with her and, at that point, through their disobedience Satan gained a legal right to operate on the earth.

When Jesus (the "second Adam" according to 1 Corinthians 15:45-47) came, His mission was to take back *for man* the authority that had been lost in the Garden. God's pleasure with this mission was obvious, for when Jesus was being baptized in water and the Holy Spirit descended upon Him, the Father said, "This is my beloved Son, in whom I am well pleased." At that point, the battle to discredit God's Word was on once again. Jesus was led into the wilderness where Satan began working on Him using the tactic of temptation. Satan proclaimed to Jesus that he had authority over everything on earth. In Luke 4:6 (amp.) Satan said to Jesus, "to you I will give all power and authority and their glory . . . for it has been turned over to me and I will give it to whom I will." Jesus' response was the same that we should be using on the devil today. He said to the devil in Luke 4:8, *"Get behind me, Satan. For it is written . . . "* Three times the enemy attacked Jesus, and each time Jesus responded with, "It is written" and then quoted the Word. That is still the way to enforce the enemy's defeat today. James 4:7 tells us that if we draw nigh to God and resist the devil he will leave us. Following Jesus' example does exactly that. When we speak the

Word, we are both drawing close to God and resisting the devil at the same time.

One particularly effective device the enemy uses that believers should be on the lookout for is the "divide and conquer" tactic. He loves to magnify differences between people causing them to become offended with each other. He operates at all levels of society. Whether it be causing disunity in marriage, resulting in divorce, racial and ethnic differences within a nation, resulting in turmoil and even war, or doctrinal differences in the Body of Christ, which result in religious schisms, the devil uses the "spirit of offense" very masterfully. Praise God, the Lord is moving on His people today to recognize this attack on the Church and on the world, and we are learning to refuse to give in to the enemy in this area.

According to 1 Timothy 2:4, God's desire is that all men be saved and come to the knowledge of the truth. That truth includes not only the fact that Jesus died to save us from our sins so we could spend eternity with Him, but also so we could spend our time in this life living in victory, sharing with others the source of our strength. And, to live in total victory, you must know that you have authority over the works of the devil. When you know that and receive that as part of the "salvation" Jesus purchased for you, John 8:32 takes on new meaning. Jesus said, "You shall know the truth and the truth will make you free."

Jesus left no doubt of what he expected from those who would choose to follow Him. His marching orders for the Church found in Luke 10:19 (amp.) leave no room for debate:

> Behold! I have given you authority and power to trample upon serpents and scorpions, and (physical and mental strength and ability) over all the power that the enemy (possesses), and nothing shall in any way harm you.

The Armor of God

David is often referred to as a man after God's heart. How can that be said about a man whose personal failures are so well-documented in the Word? The answer lies in the fact that David was an overcomer. He recognized that God's greatest desire was to see him succeed over every obstacle in his life, even those that were of David's own making. Psalms 18:28-39 (amp.) reflects the fact that David knew his strength was found in God and, as a result, could be confident of victory in any battle.

> *For you cause my lamp to be lighted and shine; the Lord illumines my darkness. For by you I can run through a troop, and by my God I can leap over a wall. As for God His way is perfect! The word of the Lord is tested and tried; He is a shield to all those who take refuge and put their trust in Him. For who is God except the Lord? Or who is a rock save our God, the God who girds me with strength, and makes my way perfect? He makes my feet like hinds' feet (able to stand firmly or make progress on the dangerous heights of testing and trouble); He sets me*

securely upon my high places. He teaches my hands to war, so that my arms bend a bow of bronze. You have also given me the shield of your salvation, and your right hand has held me up; Your gentleness and condescension have made me great. You have given plenty of room for my steps under me, that my feet did not slip. I pursued my enemies and overtook them; neither did I turn again till they were consumed, I smote them so they were not able to rise; they fell wounded under my feet. For you have girded me with strength for battle; you have subdued under me and caused to bow down those who rose against me.

The total reliance David placed in God for his strength and his determination to defeat his enemies should be an example to us of how to win the battles we face. In addition, we have greater access to the power of God today than David did during his life. In Old Testament times the Holy Spirit came upon people from time to time, but today we have the Holy Spirit living within us to continually lead and guide us through every battle we face.

God created man to win, to succeed in every area of his life. His Word makes bold statements about the level of success believers are to experience. Philippians 4:13 states that we can do "all things" through Him. He said we are "more than conquerors" through Him in Romans 8:37. In Revelation 2 and 3 the Lord always uses the phrase "he who overcomes" when addressing the churches. It is very clear that the Lord expects us to overcome the devil. The Word says that Jesus is seated at the right hand of God expecting His enemies to be made His footstool. This can only happen when His Body (the Church) takes the authority and power God has given to it and exercises it over all the works of the enemy.

God never expects his children to do anything without first providing for them a way to do it. In Ephesians 6, God's provision for overcoming the enemy is revealed. I can recall one morning over twelve years ago when I asked the Lord to teach me about the "weapons of our warfare" spoken of in Ephesians. At that time I had never heard anyone teach on them. It was so wonderful how the Holy Spirit led me in a study of the different pieces of armor and how to use them. Little did I know that I would need them desperately just a short time later.

At that time our youngest daughter, Barbara, was a teenager. She had called me to her room to say good night as she normally did. But on this evening I could see that she was very upset. I asked her what was wrong and she told me she had been having nightmares. She asked me to pray with her about them. Before praying I wanted to know the nature of the nightmares. Barbara seemed reluctant to tell me. Finally she began crying and said, "Mom, I had a dream that you died and it seemed so real." After praying with her and comforting her I left the room not thinking anything more about it.

Two days later, early in the morning, I experienced a very sharp pain in my chest. It would come and go, becoming more intense each time. Because I was taking care of a friend's daughter at the time, I decided to call my daughter Pat, who lived down the street, to come over and stay with the child. When she arrived I went into the bedroom to lay down. As I lay there the Lord reminded me about the weapons about which He had been teaching me. In a short time the attack increased to the point that I could hardly breathe. As difficult as it was, I forced myself to confess 1 Peter 2:24, that I was healed by the stripes of Jesus! Pat continued to check on me and decided to call another friend who lived close by to watch my friend's daughter should it become necessary to take me for medical help. After a while I began to feel faint so Pat called my husband Ernie at work to alert him. He told her to get an ambulance and he would meet us at the hospital. The ambulance arrived quickly, and in a short time we were at the hospital. As the ambulance backed into the emergency entrance I remember thinking that I didn't know whether I could live much longer with this pain. But I continued to confess the Word of God. Ernie had arrived earlier and was there as the ambulance attendants opened the doors to move me inside. I asked the attendants to let Ernie pray for me before they took me in. The moment he laid his hands on me and began praying the pain stopped. I felt completely normal again. The attendants took me into the hospital where I was kept for a couple of hours while tests were conducted. Every test was negative. Doctors could find nothing wrong. I remember feeling so grateful to the Lord, because I believe if I had not known how to use the weapons He has provided I would surely have died that day.

That afternoon when my friend came to pick up her daughter I shared the events of the morning with her. Her response startled me. She said, "You know Eleanor, I think the devil tried to kill you." It seemed so strange that she would say that, because at that time Christians seldom talked about the devil. But when she said that, it immediately brought to mind the nightmare that Barbara had experienced a couple nights earlier. Again, I was so thankful to the Lord for showing me what to do just in time.

The weapons that God has provided for us in Ephesians 6 are full of his mercy and loving kindness. A close look at each weapon reveals that they not only protect us, but they also give us power over any situation:

Verse 10: "Finally, my brethren, be strong in the Lord and the power of His might" This verse shows us that it is not our power, but God's power, that is responsible for our overcoming. Learning about that power can come from only one place––the Living Word of God!

Vs. 11 and 12: "Put on the whole armor of God, that you may be able to stand against the wiles of the devil. For we do not wrestle against flesh and blood, but against principalities, against powers, against the rules of the darkness of this age, against spiritual hosts of wickedness in the heavenly places." These verses make clear who the enemy is. The Amplified translation for verse 11 states, ". . . that you may be able successfully to stand up against (all) the strategies and deceits of the devil." The devil is the one responsible for all the tests, trials, and tragedies that come into our lives. The Word confirms this. James 1:13 says, "Let no one say when he is tempted, I am tempted by God: for God cannot be tempted by evil, nor does He Himself tempt anyone. James 1:17-18 reinforces this truth: "Do not be deceived my brethren, every good gift is from above, and comes down from the Father of lights, with whom there is no variation or shadow of turning." Verse 11 also tells us that if we use God's weapons correctly we will be able to successfully stand against ALL strategies of the enemy. Whether we win or lose depends solely on how much knowledge we have of God's Word and on our willingness to receive and act on the promises God has given us. Verse 12 also shows us that people are not our problem, but that it is the spiritual forces that work around and through them.

Vs. 13 and 14: "therefore, take up the whole armor of God, that you may be able to withstand in the evil day, and having done all, to stand. Stand therefore, having girded your waist with truth, having put on the breastplate of righteousness." In these verses the Apostle Paul emphasizes the importance of standing. This is necessary because tests and trials do not always come to an end as quickly as we would like them to. James 1:2-4 reinforces this idea. "My brethren, count it all joy when you FALL into various trials, knowing that the testing of your faith produces patience. But let patience have its perfect work, that you may be perfect and complete, lacking nothing. (Perfect means mature). In order to stand through the duration of the trial it is necessary to have support to hold you up. That is what the "girdle of truth" spoken of in v. 14 provides. The truth of God's Word is what holds a Christian together in good times and bad. We must daily surround ourselves with the Word—through devotions, prayer time, tapes, and music. "Girding" is a lifestyle which requires us to be more than just believers. We must be disciples, students of God's Word. The Word describes one such disciple in Psalms 1:2 (amp.) "But his delight and desire are in the law of the Lord, and on His law—the precepts, the instructions, the teaching of God—he habitually mediates (ponders and studies) by day and night."

The breastplate of righteousness in v. 14 refers to the fact that we are in a position of "right-standing" with God. That position came about the day we made Jesus Christ the Lord of our lives. We don't have to work to be righteous—it was a part of the "salvation package." Why is this a part of the armor of God? Because it protects one of the areas in which the enemy loves to attack. When we make mistakes or fall short, he loves to put condemnation on us and make us "feel" so unworthy. A breastplate is designed to protect the heart. So it is as believers we must protect in our hearts what we know is the truth of God's Word, even when our head is telling us something different. And, on the occasions when we do sin, we do what 1 John 1:9 tells us to do. "If we confess our sins, He is faithful and just to forgive us our sins and cleanse us from all unrighteousness."

Verse 15 (amp.): "and having shod your feet in preparation (to face the enemy with firm-footed stability, the promptness and readiness produced by the good news) of the gospel of peace." This means we always need to be ready to share Jesus with others, to share the good news of how God has prepared and provided a way for all people to receive His blessings by receiving His Son as Lord and Savior.

Verse 16 (amp.): "Lift up over all the (covering) shield of saving faith, upon which you can quench all the flaming missiles of the wicked (one)." Using this weapon allows us to face any struggle because of our absolute trust and confidence in the Lord's ability and desire to deliver us. One definition of faith is "believing God will do what he said He would do." In the natural a shield is something we stand behind for protection. Likewise, we should always stand behind God's Word in any situation and it will shield us. For instance, if a doctor says you have cancer and have only a short time to live, he is stating what he believes based on the results of medical tests. Faith doesn't deny the doctor's report. But faith knows the truth of God's Word supersedes the "facts." 1 Peter 2:24 says you were healed! God has provided healing through the finished work of the Cross. Of course the hard part is focusing on the Word while the enemy is attacking your body with symptoms of the disease. But the Lord even instructed us how to keep our focus on Him. In 2 Corinthians 10:3-5 it states, "For though we walk in the flesh, we do not war according to the flesh. For the weapons of our warfare are not carnal but mighty in God for pulling down strongholds. Casting down arguments (thoughts, fiery darts) and every high thing that exalts itself against the knowledge of God, bringing every thought into captivity to the obedience of Christ." It is focusing on that "knowledge of God" you have in your heart that keeps you from focusing on the symptoms you are experiencing.

Verse 17: "and take the helmet of salvation and the sword of the Spirit, which is the Word of God." We need a weapon that protects our mind, because as verse 12 says, the root of our battle is not physical, but rather spiritual. And the area that the enemy finds easiest to attack is our minds, because unlike our spirits which were recreated when we were born-again, our minds were not. The mind is where the battle is. Romans 8:7 states, "The carnal mind is enmity against God; for it is not subject to the law of God, nor indeed can it be." In Romans 7:23, Paul writes, "But I see another law in my members warring against the law of my mind, and bringing me into captivity to the law of sin which is in my members." The answer to this problem is found in Romans 12:2, "And do not be conformed to this world, but be transformed by the renewing of your mind, that you may prove what is that good and acceptable and perfect will of God." When we renew our minds on the Word of God we are doing what Peter told us to do in 1 Peter 1:13. He said, "Therefore gird up the loins of your mind, be sober, and rest your hope fully upon the grace that is to be brought to you at the revelation of Jesus Christ." In 1 Corinthians 2:16 we are told that we have the "mind of Christ"––but only if our mind is renewed on His Word continually!

The fact that the "helmet" is *salvation* takes on added significance when the original meaning of the Greek word used, "soteria," is understood. It means, "rescue or safety; deliver, health, salvation, save, saving." It goes beyond providing for eternal life. Salvation provides for victory on this side of heaven also! It is always God's will to deliver us. The "helmet" is knowing this and recalling this no matter how bleak the situation. It provides steadiness when the natural mind wants to focus on all the natural circumstances that go contrary to God's Word.

The end of v. 17 deals with the only offensive weapon of the armor––the Sword of the Spirit. This is the weapon Satan hopes you never find out about! The other weapons protect *against attacks*. The Sword of the Spirit, which is the Word of God, allows us to go *on the attack*. We do that by taking the authority Jesus gave us as believers. In Luke 10:19, Jesus said, "Behold, I give you the authority to trample on serpents and scorpions (demons) and over all the power of the enemy, and nothing shall by any means hurt you." Our job is not to defeat Satan. 1 John 3:8 says that Jesus already did that. It says, "For this purpose the Son of God was manifested, that He might destroy the works of the devil." Our job is to enforce his defeat in this world until Jesus returns. Every time the church preaches the gospel, which according to Mark 16 involves casting out devils and laying hands on the sick, it is enforcing the defeat of the devil. It is doing great damage to the kingdom of darkness. Every time the Word of God is spoken out of a believer's mouth light is brought into this dark world. Hebrews 4:12 describes just how powerful the Word of God is. It says, "For the word of God is quick and powerful and sharper than any two-edged sword, piercing even to the dividing asunder of soul and spirit, and of the joints and marrow, and is a discerner of the thoughts and intents of the heart."

The final element involved in the armor of God is found in Ephesians 6:18. *"Praying always with all prayer and supplication in the Spirit, be watchful to this end with all perseverance and supplication for all the saints."* We are told in this passage to be watchful and ready to intercede on behalf of all the Body of Christ, always prepared to build those up who are under attack. By doing that we are actually strengthening our lives for the battles that lay ahead for ourselves.

Now using the example of heart disease, this is how the armor of God works for you. The devil attacks and you've been told that you are going to die from heart disease just like your father did. You've already set the stage for victory by "putting on" the armor of God during your prayer time with the Lord:

Waist girded with truth	-you've received God's Word as truth
Breastplate of righteousness	-you've received your position of right-standing with God
Feet shod, preparation of peace	-you've received the responsibility of sharing Jesus with others
Shield of faith	-you've received God's Word and his willingness to bring it to pass in your life
Helmet of salvation	-you're renewing your mind with the Word continually
Sword of the Spirit	-you're speaking God's Word with authority over your situation
Prayer and supplication	-you're interceding for others to be victorious over their struggles

You are covered from head to toe. When the enemy tries to carry out his attack he comes against an armor that cannot be penetrated!

The Word never promised a believer a life free of tests and trials. As long as we live on this earth in flesh and blood bodies, there will be continual attacks by the enemy. But God has *promised* victory through each one of them, and has *provided* the means to do it by giving us His armor. What remains to be done is for us as believers to receive that promise and that provision by faith. The Word gives us a very vivid picture of what awaits those who dare to believe God's Word concerning the trials of life in Isaiah 43:1-3:

> *. . . Fear not for I have redeemed you; I have called you by your name; You are mine When you pass through the waters, I will be with you; and through the rivers, they shall not overflow you. When you walk through the fire, you shall not be burned, Nor shall the flame scorch you. For I am the Lord your God, The Holy One of Israel, your Savior. . .*

What Is Faith?

The Bible promises us in Matthew 7:7, if we seek we will find. My husband Ernie and I were always hungry for God and we really wanted to understand His ways. From the beginning of my Christian walk I wanted to know more about faith. Preachers told me I needed it, and I knew I would not be successful in my Christian walk without it. But my understanding of it remained a mystery for the first ten years of my Christian life.

Looking back, I now understand why. According to the Word, nothing is closer to God's heart than faith. Hebrews 11:6 says, ". . . without faith it is impossible to please God." Whenever there is a move of God in which He is bringing revelation to His Church in a certain area, the devil will be working overtime to try to stop the truth from being revealed. That is what happened when the "Faith Movement" began in the 1960s. The devil, deceived as always, really thought he could snuff out this movement by persecuting the people God had chosen to bring forth the message. But the Word cannot be stopped, and through the years the movement has grown stronger and stronger. Today the faith message is abounding everywhere.

It is no wonder that the devil was so intent on stopping this movement. At the heart of the faith movement is the "system" designed by our Heavenly Father to meet each and every need of His children. This system is called "faith." The reason it is impossible to please God without faith is because His number one desire is to bless His children, and faith is the avenue through which He has chosen to pour out those blessings!

As is the case with anything dealing with God, an understanding of faith can only come through knowing His Word. So the Word is where a believer goes to find out about faith. Hebrews 12:2 says that Jesus is the author and the finisher of our faith. Romans 10:17 says that we can only receive faith by hearing the Word of God. These two scriptures fit perfectly together because John 1:1 says Jesus was the Word. So the starting place for understanding faith is with Jesus. Receiving salvation and receiving faith came at the moment we made Jesus Lord and Savior of our lives. The Word confirms this in Romans 12:3: ". . . God had dealt to every man the measure of faith."

Understanding now that every believer has "faith," the next step in unraveling the mystery is to find out what faith actually "is." Hebrews 11:1 (amp.) gives the most conclusive definition of this term: "Now faith is the assurance (the confirmation, the title—deed) of the things we hope for, being the proof of things we do not see and the conviction of their reality-faith perceiving as real fact what is not revealed to the senses." Faith is a spiritual substance or force that connects the physical world to the spiritual world where God's power originates. It brings back to us whatever we need. Philippians 4:19 says that "my God shall supply all your need according to His riches in glory by Christ Jesus." According to Psalms 23:1 it even brings back to us our wants (as long as they line up with the Word). It says, "The Lord is my shepherd, I shall not want . . ." Faith is a spiritual law, much like gravity is a natural law. If you jump from a high building, the law of gravity will bring you to the ground. If you believe God for something in your life, the spiritual law of faith will bring it into reality.

The Word reveals that both God and the believer have a responsibility when it comes to faith. God's part is doing what He said He would do in his Word. First of all He promised He would never change. In Malachi 3:6 He says, "I am the Lord, I change not." In Psalms 89:34 it is written, "My covenant I will not break, Nor alter the word that has gone out of my lips." So His Word confirms that He is going to do what He said.

The believer's role in faith is likewise listed in the Word. The Bible tells us that the "just shall live by faith." (Galatians 3:11) According to 2 Corinthians 5:7 we "walk by faith and not by sight." Living and walking denote action. Faith is not there to be used "on occasions." Faith is a lifestyle for the Christian. Its benefits are described in 1 John 5:4: "For whatever is born of God overcomes the World. And this is the victory that has overcome the world—even our faith." When faith is present we have victory over everything that tries to bring us down.

God's promise is there to give us faith. He has shown us what part we are to play. What is needed is something that makes the connection between the spirit world and the natural world. The "switch" that activates the force of faith is our mouth. Think about it; this is how we were born-again. Romans 10:6-10 states:

> *But the righteousness of faith speaks in this way, Do not say in your heart, Who will ascend into heaven? (that is, to bring Christ down from above) or, Who will descend into the abyss? (that is, to bring Christ up from the dead). But what does it say? The word is near you, even in our mouth and in your heart (that is, the word of faith which we preach): That if you confess with your mouth the Lord Jesus and believe in your heart that God has raised Him from the dead, you will be saved. For*

> *with the heart one believes unto righteousness, and with*
> *the mouth confession is made unto salvation.*

By simply believing in our hearts and speaking that belief out of our mouths we activated salvation in our lives. In the *Strong's Concordance*, the Greek word for salvation is "soteria." It means to rescue, to provide physical and moral deliverance, to provide health, and to save. That's a bundle of blessings that can be activated by the words we speak! In 1 John 5:14-15 (amp.) we are told what to expect as we begin to speak out the blessings of God in our lives:

> *And this is the confidence—the assurance, the boldness*
> *which we have in Him: (we are sure) that if we ask*
> *anything (make any request) according to His will (in*
> *agreement with His own plan—His Word) He listens*
> *to and hears us. And if (since) we (positively) know that*
> *He listens to us in whatever we ask, we also know (with*
> *settled and absolute knowledge) that we have (granted*
> *us as our present possessions) the requests made of him.*

Now let's bring this home to where we live by using the following illustration. Say you are a born-again believer. The doctor has told you that you have cancer and have only a year to live. The tests are in and it's a fact—you do have cancer. At this point you don't deny you have it, but you do deny its right to stay in your body. Cancer is a reality, but the Word of God is Truth. In Ephesians 1:21 it says that Jesus is far above every name that is named. Cancer is just a name, and that name is beneath the name of Jesus.

From the beginning of the trial you cannot afford to entertain thoughts for one moment that God had anything to do with this disease coming on you. The devil is the author of sickness and Jesus is the author of life. (John 10:10) This truth must be settled in your mind once and for all because if you think He is behind this sickness (because He's trying to teach you something or get you to grow spiritually), you won't be able to put your full trust in Him for your deliverance.

The best way to keep your mind off the sickness is to keep it focused on the Word of God. Revelation 12:11 reveals the double-barreled weapon you are to use to enforce the enemy's defeat in your situation: "And they overcome him by the blood of the Lamb, and by the word of their testimony . . . " You have a covenant with your Father God which you gained access to by the shed blood of Jesus. That covenant goes into effect when the Word of God comes out of your mouth. According to Hebrews 4:12, the Word of God is ". . . living and powerful and sharper than any two-edged sword." This spells *victory* for you and *defeat* for the devil! Every time you confess God's promises over your body for divine healing something is happening spiritually, even if you can't see it or feel it. God's power in His Word is working on the root of the sickness, destroying it. Romans 8:11 says the Holy Spirit quickens (makes alive) our mortal bodies. God has promised us long life (Psalms 91:16). Confess Psalms 118:17: "I shall not die, but live, and declare the works of the Lord." God wants you well to carry out His destiny for you here on earth. We should continually thank God and praise Him for the healing that is ours in Christ Jesus. Our Pastor shared this nugget of wisdom one Sunday: "When you receive a miracle from God, your praise is thanksgiving. When you praise God before you see your miracle—THAT'S FAITH!"

Hebrews 11 discusses the great men and women of faith. Each one went against the natural flow of this world in order to receive from God what He had promised. Although one person cannot be singled out from the others as having had greater faith, Abraham can be singled out because the Word connects him directly with the generations of believers that will follow until Jesus' return. (Galatians 3:29) Abraham's faith is described in Romans 4:19-21:

> *And being not weak in faith, he considered not his own*
> *body now dead, when he was about a hundred years old,*

neither yet the deadness of Sarah's womb: He staggered not at the promise of God through unbelief; but was strong in faith, giving glory to God; And being fully persuaded that, what he had promised, he was able also to perform.

What was the blessing received by Abraham because of his faith stance? James 2:23 reveals the answer. ". . . Abraham believed God and it was imputed unto him for righteousness and he was called the *Friend of God*." To be called a child of God is certainly a privilege and an honor, but to be called a friend of God goes even beyond that. The first denotes relationship, the second, fellowship. Of all the blessings God wants to pour out on us, perhaps the greatest is that He just wants to be our friend––someone with whom we spend time, someone with whom we share our grandest dreams and our greatest disappointments, someone whom we just enjoy being with. This relationship is still available for every believer today, according to Galatians 3:29:

And if you are Christ's, then you are Abraham's seed, and heirs according to the promise.

How to Receive Your Healing

In the previous chapters we learned about how much God loves us and wants us to have an abundant life. We also learned how much the devil hates us and wants to destroy and kill us because of that love the Father has for us.

We saw how Jesus came and purchased everything we would need to defeat the enemy through His shed blood. The Word says that Jesus came to destroy the works of the devil! (1 John 3:8) When you became a child of God, you were given authority to use His name to enforce that defeat and be victorious over him. (Luke 10:19)

Sickness is one of the biggest weapons the devil uses to attack God's children. There is absolutely no doubt, according to the Word, that God wants you well and expects you to be healed when the enemy attacks. The Lord says in Romans 8:37 that we are more than conquerors. Philippians 4:13 states that we can do all things through Christ who strengthens us. You need not ask if it is God's will to heal you! God's Word is very, very clear on the subject. Psalms 103:2-3 says, "Bless the Lord O my soul, and forget not all His benefits; who forgives all your iniquities, *who heals all your diseases . . .*" Matthew 8:16-17 (amp.) states:

When evening came they brought to Him many who were under the power of demons, and He drove out the spirits with a word, and restored to health all who were sick; and thus fulfilled what was spoken by the prophet Isaiah, 'He Himself took (in order to carry away) our weaknesses and infirmities and bore away our diseases . . .'

1 Peter 2:24 summed it up this way: ". . . by whose stripes *we were healed!"* And just in case your head (or a well-intentioned friend) tries to tell you that those things only happened when Jesus walked the earth, Hebrews 13:8 says, "Jesus Christ is the same yesterday, today, and forever."

When the Word goes out teaching healing, the anointing is always present to heal. The Lord is always ready to heal, yet a problem sometimes arises over our ability to receive the healing. In natural terms it's like a radio receiving a message from the transmitter. If the program on the radio is fuzzy and not coming in clearly, you don't call the radio station and tell them their transmitter isn't working. You fine-tune your radio so it receives the signal the station is sending. Likewise with healing, the problem is not on the "sending" end, it's on the "receiving" end.

Let's run a checklist now to see if there could be anything standing in the way of our receiving from God. The first thing Jesus said to those who came to Him with a need was, "do not be afraid" or "fear not." You must get rid of the fear. Faith cannot operate where there is fear! 2 Timothy 1:7 says, "God has not given us a spirit of fear; but of power and of love and of a sound mind." Fear is a spirit, a force from the pit of hell that is sent to destroy God's children. You must resist Satan when he tries to bring fear on you by speaking to that spirit saying, "Fear, in the name of Jesus I resist you!" And continue to speak to the fear every time it tries to come back on you.

The next thing we must look at is unforgiveness. This is

probably one of the major reasons people do not receive that for which they are believing. God makes promises for our deliverance, but He also attaches conditions to the promises. Mark 11:24-26 illustrates that point: "Therefore I say to you, what things soever you ask when you pray, believe that you receive them, and you will have them. (That's the promise—next comes the condition). And whenever you stand praying, if you have anything against anyone, forgive him, that your Father in heaven may also forgive your trespasses. But if you do not forgive, neither will your Father in heaven forgive your trespasses."

At this time search your heart and see if there is anything that you feel could be standing between you and the Lord, that could hinder your prayer from being answered. If there is, repent and receive your forgiveness for it. He stands ready and willing to forgive you!" 1 John 1:9 says, "If we confess our sins, He is faithful and just to forgive us our sins and to cleanse us from all unrighteousness."

When we are believing to receive a promise from God's Word, there will always be a battle involved, The devil is not going to just sit back and watch the blessings of God flow into our lives. The Word calls it "the good fight of faith" (1 Timothy 6:12) The reason God calls it that is because WE WIN! Ephesians 6:10 tells us to be strong in the Lord and the power of His might. In order to do this we must have all the armor of God in place. Every piece is very important and must be put on in order to defeat the devil completely. Let's review briefly the armor that God has provided for us as revealed in His Word in Ephesians 6. (For a more detailed discussion of the armor, see Chapter Eight). The first piece of armor is the *girdle of truth*. You should totally surround yourself with the Word of God. Be careful to meditate on all of the healing scriptures. Listen to good faith—building Bible-based teaching and read books that edify and encourage you to stand strong. Next, the *breastplate of righteousness* needs to be in place. This means you receive the fact that you are in right-standing with God. Your *feet* are to be *shod with the preparation of the gospel of peace*. You need to always be ready to go——to promote the "good news" of the gospel of Christ to a dying world. Above all, according to the Word, you are to take the *shield of faith*, so you will be able to quench all the fiery darts of the wicked one. This is a stance of resistance you must maintain when the enemy is attacking. On the front of that shield there should be this message in giant letters, "NO DEVIL, I BELIEVE WHAT GOD SAYS!" The *helmet of salvation* is next. It is vital in protecting your thought-life. It involves having your mind renewed by the Word of God. If you think right, you will believe right. So as you take God's Word in your mind and heart, it will change "your way of thinking" to "God's way of thinking."

To this point the armor has been defensive in nature. Now we come to the *sword of the Spirit*, which is an offensive weapon. This involves taking the promise you have found in the Word of God that covers your situation, meditating on it until you believe it in your heart, then releasing it out of your mouth with authority. Concerning healing, the promise would be 1 Peter 2:24, ". . . by the stripes of Jesus, I am healed!" Hebrews 4:14 says that Jesus Christ is our Great High Priest and He tells us that we should hold fast to our confession. That means saying it until we see the manifestation of what we are believing for come to pass in our lives. We are to attach our hope (earnest expectation) to the Word and that produces faith. Then we "hold on" until we get results. Hebrews 10:23 says, "Let us hold fast the profession of our faith without wavering; (for he is faithful that promised)." The Word warns us that there may be a period of waiting. Ephesians 6:13-14 says, ". . . and having done all, to stand. Stand therefore . . ." The Apostle Paul is telling us that it could take time so you will need patience. No matter how long it takes, your attitude should be "I'm going to win!" Galatians 6:9 (amp.) confirms the need for patience:

> *And let us not lose heart and grow weary and faint in*
> *acting nobly and doing right, for in due season and at*

*the appointed season we shall reap, if we do not loosen
and relax our courage and faint.*

It is important that you get this fact down in your spirit—in the eyes of God you are healed! You are not the sick trying to get healed. You are the healed and the devil is trying to steal your health. But remember, Jesus has already defeated him and according to 1 John 4:4, ". . .greater is He who is in you than he who is in the world."

Once you have your armor in place, you must check to make sure you are spending time with God in prayer. You need to be listening for His direction. Proverbs 3:5-6 says:

> *Trust in the Lord with all your heart and lean not on
> your own understanding; In all your ways acknowledge
> Him, and He shall direct your paths.*

Everything on the checklist we have just reviewed has pointed, directly or indirectly, to the Word of God. That's always the place where we begin, and it is always the place where we end, when we are believing for God's provision in our life. Giving yourself totally to the Word is the final point on our checklist. Spending time in the Word is a simple task, but it is not always easy. It takes *time* and that is all too often a rare commodity in the world today. But the rewards of such diligence are life-changing as Proverbs 4:20-22, reveals:

> *My son, give attention to my words; Incline your ear to
> my sayings. Do not let them depart from your eyes; Keep
> them in the midst of your heart; For they are life to those
> who find them, and health to all their flesh.*

A Firm Foundation

What I have shared in this book has been my ongoing journey from my life as a new Christian confused by religion and the traditions of men, to the liberation I enjoy today because of the reality of God's love that I have come to experience. I realize that many of the people who read this book will have already been born-again, and like me, are searching for more in their relationship with the Lord. But I also know that there will be many who read this book who will want to receive Christ as their Lord and Savior who have not done so before. So I dedicate this last chapter to helping those who are ready to receive Jesus into their lives.

How to Become a Christian

If you have never made Jesus the Lord of your life, then you are separated from God by sin. You are the reason God sent Jesus to the cross––to pay the price for your sin, so you would not have to. John 3:16 says:

For God so loved the world, that He gave His only begotten Son, that whosoever believeth in Him should not perish, but have everlasting life.

God loves you *that much* that He gave His very best for you!

The Bible states very clearly in Romans 10:9-10 what we must do to become born of God (born-again or saved):

If you confess with your mouth the Lord Jesus and believe in your heart that God has raised Him from the dead, you will be saved. For with the heart one believes unto righteousness, and with the mouth confession is made unto salvation.

I would like to pray with you now to receive Jesus. Just repeat this out loud :

Heavenly Father, I come to you in the name of your Son, Jesus Christ. I now repent of all my sin. I pray that Jesus would be the Lord over my life. I believe that you raised Him from the dead. Jesus, please come into my heart and save me. Thank you. I now believe I'm a Christian and I will serve You all the days of my life.

After you finish saying this, begin to praise the Lord, thanking Him for coming into your life!

The next important thing for you to do is to seek the Lord for the "Baptism in the Holy Spirit." It is very important to be filled to overflowing with the Spirit of God. You must go to the Lord in faith (believing His Word) the same way you received Jesus (and the same way you receive any of the promises of God). Luke 11:9-13 tells us we are going to have to go after the things of God. They don't just come to us automatically because we've made Jesus our Lord.

And I say to you, ask, and it shall be given to you; seek, and you will find; knock, and it will be opened to you. For everyone who asks receives, and he who seeks finds, and to him who knocks it will be opened. If a son asks for bread from any father among you, will he give him a stone? Or if he asks for a fish, will he give him a scorpion? If you then, being evil, know how to give good gifts to your children, how much more will your Heavenly Father give the Holy Spirit to those who ask Him!

The Lord is reassuring us that when we ask God for something He will give us exactly what we asked for.

The Holy Spirit came to earth on the day of Pentecost. Acts 2:4 says, ". . . and they were all filled with the Holy Spirit and began to speak with other tongues as the Spirit gave them utterance." The Holy Spirit is still here today and is waiting on believers to ask Him to fill them. It is important to remember that as you pray, you are not going to rely on "feelings." You are going to receive because you have faith in what God has said. When you are baptized in the Holy Spirit the evidence of that experience is receiving a "prayer language." It is a way for your spirit to communicate with the Spirit of God. It is needed because there are things within God's Spirit and our own spirits for which there are no words in our native language. As you pray this prayer to receive the baptism of the Holy Spirit, prepare to yield to the utterances that are within you.

Now say this prayer out loud:

Dear Heavenly Father, I am a believer. I am your child and Jesus is my Lord. I believe in my heart that your Word is true. I give you my body, my mind, and my spirit. Your Word says if I ask I will receive, so I'm asking you to fill me to overflowing with your Holy Spirit. I have asked and your Word says I've received and I thank you! Now Holy Spirit, I thank you for giving me the

utterance that is my prayer language. Thank you that I
can now pray directly to the Father (1 Corinthians 14:2).

With your mouth begin to thank and praise God for filling you. As you do, certain syllables and words will rise up from within you. Stop speaking English (or your native tongue) and by faith step out boldly and speak with your new Heavenly language. (You must be willing to speak—the Lord won't force you to do it).

You are now a "spirit-filled" believer. Pray in your new language every day. It's a gift from God that enables us to speak "heart to Heart" with our Father. Remember, the Holy Spirit is always with you. He is your Comforter, your Counselor, your Helper, your Intercessor, and your Strengthener. Oh, how we need Him in the complex and dangerous world we live in.

One important step you need to take early in your walk with the Lord is to be water-baptized. This is to let the world know publicly that you are part of the Body of Christ. This is also a way for you to identify with the death, burial, and resurrection of our Lord. This is the *outward sign* of the *inward work of grace* that was imparted to you when you asked Jesus to be the Lord of your life.

Finally, make sure you ask the Lord to lead you to the church He wants you in. He will lead you to one that teaches the *uncompromising Word of God!* Become a part of what is happening there. Hebrews 10:25 admonishes us to be in fellowship with like-believers, "not forsaking the assembling of ourselves together as is the manner of some . . . ."

As you go forth now the Word says you are a "new creature in Christ." Leave your past behind you. Look only to the Word to find out "who you are" now that you are a Christian. Look only to God to find out what your future holds.

For I know the thoughts I think toward you, says the
Lord, thoughts of peace and not evil, to give you a future
and a hope. (Jeremiah 29:11)

In Conclusion

The principles of God's Word that I have shared in this book are just a portion of what God would want you to know. Through continued study of the Word, your fellowship with the Lord in daily prayer, and the leading of the Holy Spirit, you will experience an increasing knowledge and understanding of God's Kingdom and how it works. Then you, too, will be able to rejoice as I do, knowing that you are "FINALLY LIBERATED!"

Printed in the United States
By Bookmasters